Stories of Prayers & Faith

Collected and Edited
by Gloria Nye

Published by Spiral Press, R.R.5, Rockwood, ON
Canada N0B 2K0

www.spiralpress.ca

Library and Archives Canada Cataloguing in Publication

Stories of prayers & faith / compiled and edited by Gloria Nye.

ISBN 978-0-9681981-6-2

1. Christian life--Anecdotes. I. Nye, Gloria, 1938- II. Title: Stories of prayers and faith.

BV4517.S86 2010 242 C2010-901210-0

Stories of Prayers & Faith

Collected & Edited by
Gloria Nye

Assistant Editor: Alberta Nye
Cover Photograph: Micki Mahoney
Poems: Ruth Cunningham

Rockwood, ON, Canada

Enjoy! Ruth Cunningham

Only as the bird song sails
beyond the brace of budding limb
to join the faith of tender breeze
and rise in Earth's resplendent hymn

will you become composer's note
infused of trill and harmony
to fashion each tangential chorus
and strike our own divinity.

from Choice 1997

Table of Contents

The universe sings out in glee
and thrills to your humanity
so dance and drink creation's wine
rejoicing in our human time.

from The Unison of Circle

Forward

Gloria Nye

"Be glad and rejoice with all your heart."
Zeph 3:14

Many small and not-so-small miracles happen in our lives every day. I hope you enjoy this collection of such everyday miracles that ordinary people have experienced. Reading about what others have gone through can give us inspiration and courage to face our big challenges, as well as daily problems as they arise.

This volume contains twenty-six stories from twenty-two women, three men and one child. Stories written from their hearts on how prayer or faith helped them overcome obstacles they faced in their lives. Most are not professional writers, and minimal editing was done to preserve their unique voice.

One woman recalls a near fatal fall from a balcony when she was four years old. She not only survived, but experienced three other incredible happenings when angels intervened. Another woman—floating blissfully in Hawaiian waters—turns to see a shark six feet away. She too lived to write her story.

A man tells the story of his mother-in-law who, as a young bride, was found in the rubble of a London blitz blast. Her whole apartment block was destroyed, leaving only her and a glass angel figurine intact.

A daughter discovers prayer when her father has 80% of his left temporal lobe removed. She tells about his journey back—learning how to speak, walk, eat, and read all over again, and finally returning to writing lyrics and music and recording his own CDs.

A lighter hearted one is the funny story of an inebriated miner serenading an overloaded plane into the air, and there is one about how prayer helped a nine-year old girl reconcile with her best friend.

One woman finds a husband, another—her life, as she breaks away from an abusive relationship. Others battle alcohol and codependency on the way to finding themselves.

Then there is death—the death of a loved one is never easy. A woman faces her mother's passing, and my life is changed three weeks after my father died in my arms. A mother struggles to deal with the unspeakable when her teenaged son is killed. Even God seemed to forsake her, but over time her faith was renewed and she is now a comfort and support to others suffering inconsolable loss.

These and many more inspiring stories await you. Intermixed with the stories—gracing the blank pages between them—is the outstanding poetry of Ruth Cunningham. Ruth graciously consented to our using excerpts of her poetry taken from her web site and her book *Mystical Verses*. After having a taste of her incredible talent, you can dive in for more at www.self-to-self.com (Excuse the mixed metaphor.)

Thank you Ruth, and a big thank you to all the authors who opened their hearts and shared their stories. This is your book.

I welcome comments, suggestions and feedback. Email and surface mail addresses are at www.spiralpress.ca

I can think of no better way to conclude this forward than with lines from Ruth's poem, *The Unison of Circles*.

Your seeking heart returned to find
our sound-prints written in your mind
your timorous tongue speaks forth our name and
through your words we live again.

Every self will learn its lessons
every heart itself translate
in common purpose, granted freely
hailed as choice or railed as fate.

from Jan. 11, 1987

A Promise Kept

Valerie Bannert

"Ask and it shall be given you.
Seek and ye shall find." Lu 11:0

For some time, I had been wanting to find a location in the country to develop and grow into a special place of retreat. I was looking for a place, not only for myself, but a special dwelling that I could share with others who needed the country in their lives.

First, I started reading about properties for sale. It had to be near enough for me to commute to St. Sebastian's School in Toronto's west end, and, after eliminating vacation country, I thought I might explore the Terra Cotta area. There was a river there, and water was a must.

I believed that I had a hint of a promise, and considering the Source, it would be a promise that would be kept. I packed a lunch for my pup, Kenji, and me, and off we went—headed west. It was a feeling akin to preparing to go fishing with mom and dad. You wonder, not if you will catch any fish, but how many and how big.

In high spirits and with great expectancy, we headed for the Terra Cotta countryside, driving on both main and back roads. I saw nothing. Nothing even close. I knew what I was looking for and I knew that I would know it when I saw it.

By late afternoon, my spirits had lagged and the thought occurred to me to drive to my favourite area near Eden Mills. We could sit in the woods there and finish our lunch before returning to the city.

I turned off the Guelph Line onto Indian Trail and stopped just before a little bridge where we parked in the Spirit Valley Farm driveway. After walking a bit into the woods, we finished the rest of our lunch, then headed back to the car. As I turned around ready to leave, I thought, *Where, oh where, is the promise?*

I nosed the car onto Indian Trail and for some reason, hesitated. I had been out this way many times before, yet had never crossed that little bridge. Why not just drive over it and then turn around to head back to the city?

Half way across, I stopped on the bridge—it was more like I was stopped on the bridge. Something simply grabbed me. There was no other way to explain it. I looked up the river at the tiny island lush with cedars, and then down the river at the water lapping and dancing in silver glory. My heart sang, half in sadness and half in total awe. I don't know if I said it aloud or just in my depths, but it was, *Oh, God, there must be some place for me!* Then I corrected myself. I remember it so clearly. *No, not just for me but for others.* Something grabbed my spirit. As I prayed, I felt that I belonged there.

I took a deep breath and continued over the bridge to turn around. At the end, on the property to the right was a sign and on the sign, printed in large red letters were the words: For Sale.

I drove to the gate, scrambled out, and, ignoring threatening signs, Kenji and I crawled through a fence, and followed what once had been a driveway. Through the dense growth of trees, I saw, just slightly visible ahead, an old log bungalow.

Kenji and I ran toward it and then around to the back, where we found a terrace that sloped down to the gentle Eramosa River. Two or three cabins peeked through the woods.

"Oh, look at that, Kenji," I cried. A three story, octagonal, tiered building smiled upon our astonished gaze and seemed to fold us in its loving embrace. Kenji sprang to life, racing back and forth on the lawn, into the river and back to the lawn as if getting my consent to claim territory. He was smiling and so was I. We were not claiming—we were being claimed. We had come home. The promise was kept.

Through the years, as I continue to delight in Eramosa Eden (www.eramosaeden.org) I often ask, "Okay, God, what did I do to deserve this?" I always rejoice in the very firm response. "Nothing, nothing at all. It is simply my gift."

Spoken through the living moment
Self-to-self and each to all
conversations through the centuries
answer to each seeker's call

from Jan. 11, 1987

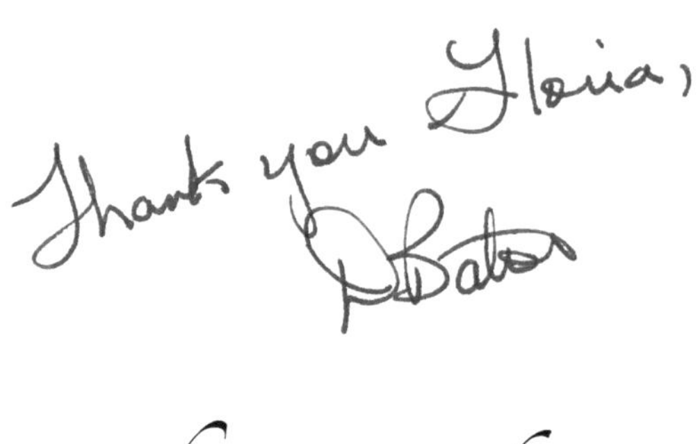

Gifts from God

Diane Bator

"Fear not, for I am with thee: turn not aside, for I am thy God. I have strengthened thee, and have helped thee, and the right hand of my just one hath upheld thee."
Isaiah 41:10

I vividly remember sitting in the waiting area in the surgical unit of the hospital watching my mom struggling with a crossword puzzle. It was a futile effort. There was only one thing on our minds and it did not involve words—across or down. My dad, Joe, lay in an operating room down the hall with his skull wide open.

Prayer was never something we did as a family, but it was something I did every minute after he entered Foothills Hospital. I recited the only prayer I knew "Our Father who art in heaven, hallowed be thy name." Besides my family, The Lord's Prayer was all I had to keep me strong.

We didn't know Dad was epileptic until the winter I was sixteen and a doctor diagnosed him with Complex-Partial Epilepsy. This came as a huge blow. My dad was very active, being an avid hunter and trapper. He also owned a sawmill and loved to dabble in music. When I was little, he built his own sawmill and cut trees to clear space for fields and housing developments using only his skidder. He also volunteered on the board of directors of two apartment buildings for seniors. In the evenings, he played his electric guitar, however, it wasn't long before my Mom would banish him and it to the heated shed out back .

Over the next six or seven years, he tried one medication after another, including experimental drugs, but nothing eased the seizures. His last chance for a normal life was surgery. His operation lasted ten hours, an agonizing wait for those of us who had to sit on our hands and do nothing. My mom, my brother, and I tried to do puzzles or carry on conversations but it was difficult to focus. The odds of him recovering completely, after having eighty percent of his left temporal lobe removed, were not in Dad's favour. A quarter-sized section of his brain would be gone forever.

He returned to his hospital bed with forty-seven stitches holding his scalp tog nbether. He couldn't remember his own name let alone ours, but from the lopsided grin that covered his face, we knew he was happy to see us.

I went home that night and cried. Although my brother and I weren't raised to be religious people, we both knew the power of prayer, and the need to have faith that he would heal.

Slowly, Dad's brain forged new connections, and, despite doctor's orders to stay in bed, he often snuck over to a chair by the window. He began to remember names: ours, all of his nurses, and his own. I still remember crying the first time he called me Dee, which had been his nickname for me since I was a baby. Fifteen days after surgery, he went home to begin rehabilitation.

Over the next two-and-a-half years, my dad relearned how to talk, how to associate words with objects, and how to read and write. Even feeding himself was a struggle, since his right hand refused to do what he wanted it to do. The part of his brain that housed his musical ability remained intact, but he couldn't sing or play his guitar with an uncooperative hand. Never one to back down from a fight, however, Dad took this as just one more thing to work through.

It has been seventeen years since my father's brain surgery; he is considered a medical miracle. The odds were astronomical that he would recover completely from the surgery that could have left him in a vegetative state or taken his life.

My dad has had other challenges that never got him down. His lungs have been damaged from a gas well blow out. His body has been ravaged by time and accidents. He has arthritis in his knees, and pain in his back from an injury to his neck. Spinal cord damage has left him unable to lift and carry things, but even with all that, he is happy.

My dad not only records his own CDs and sells them at farmers' markets, he also writes his own lyrics and music. Last fall, he recruited me to help him with some lyrics, and between the two of us, we have created four CDs, with one more on the way in 2010. I have my father back and he has his amazing talent despite all odds.

Over the years, I've written several books that I hope to see published. When I get rejections, I don't feel beaten, because on my shelf are my dad's sixteen CDs. I look at them and know that, with a little faith, I can make my dreams come true if I follow my father's example and use the gifts God gave me.

From One Angel to another - Thanks be to God. Freda Turner. April 4th/2010.

My Mother's Angel

George A. Brooks

"For He shall give His angels watch over thee, to keep thee in all thy ways." Ps. 91:11

The bombs fell upon the city of London with the frightening whistle of death. It was early spring of 1940 and the Battle of Britain raged around a newly married 21 year old young woman.

My mother-in-law, Freda, had come from the north of England to London in 1936 at age 16 to find work. She was young, vibrant and strong willed and had convinced her mother back in Newcastle that she would be fine—plus there were no jobs locally. In London, she worked long hours as a nanny, looking after three children and doing light housekeeping. Then she met a young man named Les who delivered groceries to local homes. They became friends and were soon dating. She was now 17 but level headed enough to know that she was too young to marry. The courting continued, and she became engaged at age 20, and they were married in a small church in London, England. By this time Les had joined the army and was being trained for the African front. When the war started, Freda took on a job at a nursing hospital for wounded soldiers. She often stayed late into the evening to talk to the soldiers and listen to their stories about home and loved ones. She showed great compassion and Christian love for the wounded and dying in her charge.

It was a Friday evening in September 1940, when Freda hurried home to her second story apartment on Watford Way in London. She was very tired after a week of work at the hospital. Although exhausted, she was excited because her husband Les was coming home for a weekend leave.

The ship that was to take him to Africa was overloaded, so he and several soldiers had not been able to embark. That very troop ship was torpedoed after it left port with the loss of all on board.

Freda had a light meal, cleaned up the kitchen, dusted the three little rooms in the apartment and made the bed up, deciding not to sleep in it, so that it and the room would stay neat for Les' arrival. She closed the heavy blackout curtains and turned on one dim light. Then she sat in a living room chair and read from her Bible until drifting off to sleep. She remembered dreaming of her wedding day the previous February and the precious gift her mother had given her. It was an angel figurine made of frosted pale blue crystal standing in the centre of a glass bowl—not expensive, but precious because it had belonged to her grandmother. When she was a little girl she had watched her mother fill the bowl with flowers or fruit. Back then, when she looked at the crystal angel, it seemed to smile, which, in some strange manner, calmed and encouraged her. Time and time again, while growing up, she experienced this.

In her dream that particular night, she recalls the angel hovering above her and whispering, "I will keep you safe."

That September 17 was a devastating night of destruction in London. The first flight of German bombers attacked just after midnight, and the noise of exploding bombs and screaming sirens awakened Freda. She looked up at the angel sitting on the fireplace mantel and a feeling of calm came over her. Again, she felt safe and secure. The bombers moved away and the sirens stopped their wail. After several minutes of listening to the night return to quiet, she moved to the living room couch and soon fell back to sleep.

From the French coast, a second wave of German bombers was launched. They flew from their runways with a vengeance and deadly purpose. In less than an hour, they were over London and started dropping their load of horror. One of the planes flew across the district of Mill Hill, unloading bombs down the line of tenement houses in which Freda lived. The horrifying explosives tore through several stores and apartment houses. As the plane moved away, the screams of people joined the screams of the sirens, with people calling out for loved ones. Within minutes, the wardens and first aid workers were scrambling through the rubble to identify the living and the dead.

"Here mate," yelled an ambulance worker to the warden, "looks like a young married woman's arm. I can see a new ring on her left hand."

The warden knew of the newly wed bride in 3B. "Freda is her name," he said and looked up at her building. It was half destroyed by a jagged piece of stone wall that had fallen from the adjacent building and was now leaning against the outside stairwell of her apartment. Part of the upstairs was destroyed. The warden ran to the stairs and carefully, began to climb up. The stairs creaked and shook as he made his way to what was left of Freda's apartment. At the top of the stairs he could see that the bedroom had been blown away and his heart sank. The arm and hand with the ring buried in the rubble below must be Freda's. The door from the stairs to the living room was blown off its hinges. The warden looked in and called into the darkness "Freda,

Freda, are you there?"

There was no answer and the warden cautiously stepped into the living room, expecting the floor to give way at any moment. He flashed his torch around the room.

The large living room window was blown in and the heavy drapes lay in shreds on the floor. The fireplace and mantel were now leaning outwards, against a weakened wall ready to fall. His torch light again lit up the bundle of ripped curtains on the floor. There was someone or something under the rubble of glass shards and curtains. The warden got to his hands and knees and slowly moved towards the pile of debris. Something flashed brightly above the bundle as his torch light played across it. It was a strange light, more of a glow with a bluish radiance and for some reason the warden felt encouraged by the sight, and he called out, "Freda, Freda, are you all right?"

Freda had not heard the explosion. The blast from the bomb had shattered the window sending hundreds of shards of glass into the heavy curtain. Freda was thrown to the floor as the heavy curtain, mangled with glass, landed on her. She fell to the floor unconscious and bleeding from several superficial cuts that miraculously had only scratched her arms and the side of her neck.

More than twenty minutes had passed since the falling wall from the explosion had destroyed her apartment and she was just starting to come to when she heard a voice in the distance. "Freda, Freda, are you all right?"

She thought to herself, *what is a man doing in my bedroom?* As she tried to yell, only a dry croak came out, "Don't come near me, I'm in my dressing gown."

"Freda, there's been an explosion, I'm the warden and I have to get you to safety."

Freda gradually took in the enormity of what had happened. With daylight emerging, she could see sky where her bedroom used to be. She started to sit up when she realized that she was holding the crystal angel in her hand.

Looking around the room and at the mantel, she could see that everything was destroyed including the crystal bowl that lay in pieces at her feet. Only Freda and her angel had survived. Her dream drifted into her mind "I will keep you safe" and she cried as she thanked her Lord for His protection.

It was a slow and frightening descent, with the warden gently holding Freda's arm as they came down the shaking stairs to the street level. While a medic was treating her cuts, she turned her head to see the stairs and back wall of her home collapse in a shower of dust and smoke. Looking down at her angel that she held tightly against her bosom, she again, lifted up a prayer of thanks.

Freda survived the war as did her husband Les. She survived the trials and tribulations of raising a child on her own for five years while her husband fought in far off Egypt.

She survived the trip to the new world when she and her husband and two children came to Canada. They arrived in Sudbury, Ontario in September of 1947 and she survived that too! She survived running a boarding house to add to the family income, and she survived the loss of her husband Les, and years later the loss of her Canadian husband, Maurice, also a decorated war veteran.

When things got difficult and life's problems seemed insurmountable, she turned her eyes to her crystal angel and prayed. Life always seemed a little easier after these moments of prayer and angel contemplation.

Freda is a widow now and the angel sits on the mantel in her retirement apartment in St.Catharines, Ontario. She enjoys life in her community especially her friends and the church services on Wednesdays and Sundays. She has her children, her grandchildren, and great grandchildren who bring her joy and satisfaction.

Freda is 91 years old now, and there are days of pain, loneliness and sadness. It is at these times that she takes down her beloved angel and holds it to her bosom and remembers the message in her dream. "I will take care of you" and she smiles and nods her head.

"I will be fine" she says to herself as she drifts off to sleep, sitting in her favourite chair to dream once more.

You grow your reasons ripe in time
like wisdom's flowers upon life's vine
you do all this, forgetting how
you grow tomorrow out of now

from The Unison of Circles

Ask, Believe, Receive

Lisa Browning

"I will lift up mine eyes unto the hills, from whence cometh my help." Ps 121:1

This quote has always meant a lot to me, for a number of reasons. First, it reminds me of *The Sound of Music*, which has always been a source of inspiration for me. (Timely, now that the stage play that I was privileged to see is coming to a close in Toronto.) In that scene Maria is advised not to fear, but to embrace life, and her destiny, wholeheartedly.

I love being in nature. It calms me, and allows me to think. Many a time have I sat under the trees in my favourite neighbourhood park, waiting for God's answer to whatever my challenge of the day might be. And the answer always came, giving me undeniable knowledge of the direction I should take.

It was during one of these times in the park that I was led to a group of people who, like me, wanted to change their lives.

Having been unhappy and unfulfilled for many years, living alone and pay-cheque to pay-cheque, I decided that I needed to make a change. Hope is an amazing thing, because it allows us to do things that we might not otherwise ever do.

Through that group, three amazing things happened:

1. After being single for over ten years following the breakdown of my marriage, I met a wonderful man, with whom I am now sharing, and building, a life.

2. I launched a freelance editing career after meeting the well-known Canadian painter Paul Duff, whose autobiography I recently published.

3. My partner and I just bought a beautiful new home in Breslau, and are anxiously awaiting a December move-in date.

I recently came across a scrap of paper on which, during a particularly difficult time in my life, I had written down the following three goals:

1. To meet a man with whom I can share my life.

2. To establish a successful freelance writing and editing career.

3. To buy a house in a country setting.

No one can ever truly know the heart and soul of another. It was not so much the circumstance in which I found myself, but rather the damage to my spirit, and my overall sense of defeat, that was most threatening. But I learned, by the grace of God, to believe that anything is possible. I learned to relax and let life happen as it is meant to happen.

As cliché as it may sound, were it not for my willingness to take a dramatic leap of faith, I never would have found myself truly living the life of my dreams.

You have felt us brush the tangles
of your cares, from weary heart
and known our love's sweet mending solace
as you braved each effort's start

from Mystical Verses

This the day of everlasting
This the moment of your grasp
this ecstatic exaltation
answer to what you have asked.

Now the day of excavation
this the task of every soul
to discover its creation,
this the truth you each extol.

from Conversion

Someone Was Watching Over Me

Michael Butler

". . . so will I watch over them . . ." Jer 31:28

It took about 45 minutes to get from my country home to my High School in the city. I was a sleepy seventeen year old, so a nap was in order. The driver usually announced my stop . . . today he forgot. The next thing I knew I was at the bus terminal in downtown Hamilton a full 12 blocks from my school.

It was 8:40 a.m. I had 20 minutes to get to class. I began my journey like a good soldier—walk briskly, but do not run. I was making incredible time, a block every 90 seconds. I might just make it. Three blocks to go and now I was moving, I was going to make it after all. I glanced to my left—there was St. Patrick's cathedral. I always liked that church, I thought.

As I approached the intersection I could see the light was going to turn green in my favour, just as all the others had. As usual, Providence was on my side. I hit the intersection in full stride, then suddenly I was jolted to a stop dead in my tracks. It was as if someone stood in front of me and struck me hard in the chest with both hands. In the blink of an eye a car sped through on a red light right in front of me.

If I had taken one more step, it would have sent me several hundred feet down the street and probably killed me.

It took a moment for me to gather my thoughts and decipher what had happened. My chest hurt as I staggered the last few blocks to school, still a little bewildered.

I stumbled into the school chapel to say a prayer of thanks. One good thing about being a dogan (Irish Catholic) in the 1960s, you were never far from one of God's houses. We had one right in the school.

I told the office I had fallen asleep on the bus and they gave me a slip to get back to class. My first class was religion as it always was in those days .

Father Holcroft greeted me at the door in his usual fashion. "Look what Providence blew in the door—albeit 20 minutes late!"

And I said back, "Father, you have no idea."

Just Ask

Elizabeth Paddon Copeland

"And I say unto you,
Ask, and it shall be given to you." Luke 11:9

Faith has been a cornerstone in my life. Through prayer I have found the courage to lift my eyes up from struggles that appear to be enveloping me and see the big picture of my life and the blessings that are mine. In my life as a single parent, I have been through cycles of poverty and recovery many times over, but none so bad as the winter of 2006.

Let me take you back. In the spring of 2004 I fell ill. I work freelance which means no work = no money coming in. Luckily, I had a bit of a financial cushion, which allowed some breathing space. I was ill most of the summer and into the fall, and I had to adjust to medications that were initially as difficult to deal with as the illness itself. By late fall I had recovered enough to go back to work, though keeping us fiscally afloat that winter was a challenge. However, with faith, hard work, deep breathing and being on every prayer list I could find, we got through.

Spring of 2006 found me with a moderately successful business that wove together my work as a performing artist/educator with that of a corporate presentation skills coach. This rather odd combination has brought me satisfaction and provided me the ability to give back to those in my community. For a decade I had worked in a Christian community with psychiatric survivors and people marginalized by poverty, using song, drama and story as a way to worship and affirm. I was the music director in a local church, worked in the schools as an arts educator and coached people in the corporate world. Though I wasn't raking it in, I was paying the mortgage and putting food on the table for my beautiful teenage daughter, Faith, our two cats and myself.

Then I got sick again. Part of working freelance means there is as much work generating it, as there is doing it, so as I was healing, I lost several opportunities. This time I had no financial cushion, but I didn't fret too much, because I knew that I had enough work booked to get us through the winter. And I had faith—or so I thought.

In October, however, just as I was getting back on my feet, I lost two big contracts—one representing half my income. As I was scrambling to try to replace the income I had lost, the financial stress sent my newfound health into a tailspin, and before you know it I was so ill I could barely function. As the months passed and less and less money flowed in, I realized I was perilously close to having to declare bankruptcy and with it came the thought of having to uproot my daughter and me. How would we survive? I needed to be healthy, and I needed money—fast.

So on one cold February night, after a great deal of weeping and gnashing of teeth, I bowed my head in prayer.

"Dear God …"

The words stuck in my throat. I could not find a place of peace inside myself with which to pray. I had to be honest with myself. I was angry— angry with God. I had reached rock bottom and I could see no way up.

I felt a fire begin to rise up in me and I sat up straight and called upon my Celtic ancestry, praying as I supposed a warrior might pray—ferociously. With my face wet with tears, I spoke to God. My voice ripped out, strangled . . . no quiet supplication here.

"I am so frustrated! I have been a good person. I have tried to do good works in this world. I have been generous with my time and talents. You can't want me to go through this."

I beat on the bed.

"Help me! You <u>will</u> help me! You will not leave my daughter and me to suffer this fate! Do you hear me!"

With my anger spent, I began to list my needs.

" *I need a job NOW—a regular job that pays good money, I have many debts to pay. I need my health restored completely! NOW. RIGHT NOW. Don't leave me here, I'm telling you. Don't."*

After blowing my nose, I added, *"And by the way, I'd also like my soul mate if you please. I'm 50 and I've waited long enough. Send him now. Thank-you. Amen"*

I fell into an exhausted sleep.

Two days later, I was offered a well paying job. It was not exactly my heart's desire, but it was work I knew I would enjoy, and that would allow me to be of service to others. The job didn't start for several weeks, which allowed me a period to rest and regain my health. Within a year, I was able to bank some money, and pay off my debts. Two months later at a wedding, I met my soul mate, Glenn. We were married this past July and have just come back from our honeymoon.

If I learned anything from that experience it was this. God wants me to make my needs clear—to not be afraid to claim my birthright as a child of God. To know that my prayers will always be heard and answered, perhaps not in the literal way they were answered on that cold February night, but answered nonetheless.

As a child growing up in the Anglican Church, I remember reciting, " *We are not worthy to gather up the crumbs under thy table.* " I think I took that too literally, and in my prayers had been asking to only be thrown a crumb here and there. I suppose I felt much like a child whose parents withhold love, and then get used to not expecting much from life. What I know now is that God is like a parent who wants to shower me with blessings and who thinks only of my highest good. Now when I pray I ask for the whole loaf of bread! What's the worst that can happen? God can say no, and love me still. *Ask and it shall be given to you.* Then pay attention. You never know how the answer will come.

Serenity Prayer

Author unknown

God grant me the serenity
to accept the things I cannot change;
Courage to change the things I can
and wisdom to know the difference;

Living one day at a time;
Enjoying one moment at a time;
Accepting even hardship
as a pathway to peace;
Taking absolutely every occurrence
in this world as it is,
not as I would have it;

Trusting that God makes all things of Love
as I surrender to God's will;
That I be reasonably happy now in this life,
and supremely happy with God forever now.

Amen

The Triumph of the Human Spirit

Lynn Emerson-Walsh

"For God has not given us a spirit of fear and timidity, but of power, love, and self-discipline." 2 Ti 1:7

The Serenity Prayer, of all Twelve-Step groups, saved my life. "God grant me the serenity to accept the things I cannot change; the courage to change the things I can; and the wisdom to know the difference."

Accept the things I cannot change, helped me to realize that my attempts to rescue others from their destructive behaviors or enable them, by spending my time, energy or money to continue bad behaviors, only prolonged their use, abuse and harmful patterns. By my trying to fix other people's problems, I neglected my own self-care and eventually depleted my own energy and resources.

The Courage to change the things I can, made me realize that my feelings, actions and reactions, ideas, behaviors, decisions, self-care and my life choices were the only things I did have control over and were solely my responsibility. While I might be responsible *to* others, I was not responsible *for* others. I came to believe it was rather arrogant of me to think I knew better what was best for another person, and if they didn't experience the full consequences of their behavior, they would never learn their lessons. And to take full responsibility for my life took courage!

The wisdom to know the difference, was a challenge to grow emotionally, and learn to love unconditionally; to become completely honest with myself and speak my truth to others; to recognize that peace and serenity come from within; to realize a better future came about by daily making good choices; and it was important for me to think things through before making decisions or taking action.

I realized that taking full responsibility for my life and not blaming others; making amends for my mistakes, except when it would cause harm to another or myself; forgiveness of others and ultimately myself; prayer and meditation; and being of service to others, are the spiritual foundation of all Twelve-Step programs

As I recovered from alcohol abuse and unhealthy relationships, I repeated this prayer over and over when crisis gripped my life. Moment by moment, day-by-day, God's loving power balanced and harmonized my life and attuned me to my higher purpose. By understanding the root causes of my addictions; by living a more honest and authentic life; and by allowing my God-given gifts and talents to surface, I found a more meaningful connection with our Creator, the loving force that heals us when we remain open to our divine nature.

As my relationship with God and my prayer life deepened, magical things started to happen. I believe humanity is waking up, ego-based agendas are transforming into a higher consciousness, the triumph of the human spirit is being felt globally, and the force of love is overcoming fear. For where there is fear there can be no love and where there is love there can be no fear.

Filling up the heart's deep river
swifter roars the flow of time
on its foaming crest there quivers
every dreamer's dream divine.

from Jan. 12, 1987

A Nest of Cardinals

Helga Farrant

"Blessed are those who have not seen, but believe."
Jn. 20:29

Snow was still melting under the pine trees when the timid cardinals made their nest. They carefully gathered twigs and winter weary bits of long grass, building it into an old tall rose shrub which grew along my fence. Soon three eggs were in it. Then I heard peeping sounds. The eggs had hatched.

Later, while the mother was away gathering food, I climbed up my little ladder, camera in hand, hoping to get a photo of the newborns. But she was back instantly, diving at me and squawking loudly. I only managed one quick look before I was shooed away.

Crowded in the nest, were three little birds—mostly naked, with a few bits of down and tiny feeble wings. Pink eyelids still covered their unseeing eyes. On hearing the sound of their mother's wings, they peeped loudly, and eagerly stretched out their scrawny necks in her direction.

With beaks gaped opened for food, and without being able to see her at all, somehow, they recognized their mother and trusted her. Hour by hour she faithfully fed her little ones and within a few days they grew strong enough to open their eyes.

Someone told me once that we too are like these tiny helpless birds when we are born of God. Our eyes are not able to see our heavenly Father clearly. He personally watches for any threat against us and protects us. If we will open our mouths and trust him to nourish us, we will be fed good things and we will grow. In time, our eyes will open to see him more and more clearly.

Had the nestlings waited to see if it was really their mother before taking her food, they would have died. If they had waited to see if the food was to their approval before taking it, they would have died, too. Even though good table manners insist that we be polite and not greedy, how different are these hungry little birds.

The kingdom of God is different too. God is happy when we open our mouths and hungrily and greedily ask for more of his nourishment. We are blessed and filled when we hunger and thirst after righteousness (Mt. 5:6). We are promised that we will find God if we earnestly knock and seek and ask from Him (Mt. 7:7).

When we are born in the kingdom of God, he places within our spirit his own DNA that will never die. It is His own eternal life, and we will be like him, even though at first we may seem tiny and helpless.

Our heavenly Father treasures us immensely and he will not leave us nor forsake us. Trusting Him allows Him to care for us and nurture us so that we grow strong, open our eyes, and one day, soar up into all He has for us.

Safe within our care we keep you
Self's protection— safe for all
tucked within your precious present
deep within your dream's recall

from Mystical Verses

You spin your seasons year-on-year
you brew a storm in every tear
you draw a breath, exhale a sigh
to blow the clouds cross painted sky.

from The Unison of Circles

Little Boy Pebble

Kathy Grandia

"A gift opens the way for the giver and ushers him into the presence of the great." Pr 18:16

My daughter took her gifts of knowledge, ability and time to serve as a nurse with Mercy Ships for four months in the port of Dakar, Senegal. Many months before the ship arrived, people, after walking long distances, lined up sometimes for hours to be accessed for eligibility for free treatment. This ship specialized in facial and eye surgeries and came fully equipped with surgical suites and skilled medical staff.

My daughter told me this story about a baby, just under a year old, who had been born with congenital cataracts and came to them blind. After a simple procedure, the eye pads were slowly removed as he leaned into his mother's arms. He opened his eyes and quietly put light to what he had only felt before. He lay silent for a moment and then looked at his raised hand, turning it over and around, over and around.

Then behind his hand he saw his mother's face. He became transfixed, and a look of absolute awe shone through him as he continued to hold her eyes with his.

All of those watching could imagine his brain being flooded with a new dimension—this gift of sight becoming at that moment like something sacred. His mother wept. Her black eyes drank in all that this meant for the future of her son and herself.

And the circle of the gift widened. The doctor and staff present were reminded that what they do makes a difference. In that moment, the gift the little boy had received taught them, that this is how you look at things. This is how you live wonder.

And the circle of the gift widened. Like a pebble on a pond it seemed to be saying, "Here little boy is a gift. With it comes more independence. You will be able to move more easily in safety and freedom. Colours will be real and definable. You will fit in better. You will see the sky and birds and many things that were beyond your feeling world. This gift will open up opportunities for jobs and sports and will allow you to see your own babies one day. The gift you received gave those who beheld your first moments of sight, a beautiful memory, and because you have it, you are able to see them cry—cry for the joy found in what they could give and the joy found in what you graciously received. As you received, they received, and the circle keeps widening."

As the mother wept, doctor and nurses wept. Everyone present wept—except the Little Boy.

"See, Little Boy. This is what tears of joy and relief and wonder and gratitude look like. See, Little Boy, see."

Explore your heart's capacity
to open onto meadows sweet
that stretch beyond your living sight
past broken trust, past life's defeat

from Sept. 2000

You hang the stars each night anew
you form each dream you journey through
you chase the moon on fragile wing —
when caught it answers not a thing.

from The Unison of Circles

Searching for Mr. Right*

Kim Sherman Grove

"And my God shall supply all your needs . . ."
Phil 4:19

There was much advice from friends. "Take courses at night school." "Get out more." "Go to plays and movies." "Eat at the cafeteria at work."

The one I liked best was, "You should just stop looking. When I stopped looking for someone, I met my husband."

So I would say to myself, "I'm not looking." But really, I knew that I was and that I longed to meet someone I was compatible with.

It wasn't until later that I saw what was wrong with my thinking. I had been struggling for at least five years with this desire to be married and it wasn't going away. It was by turning to God that I was guided to examine my approach to the problem.

It was like waiting to win the lottery. I started to see how much I was trusting in chance. I would go to a social gathering, wondering if this would be the day I was going to win the jack pot. Even the guy beside me at the grocery counter might have the number that matched mine. It wasn't until I saw the similarity to this kind of thinking and the lottery mentality that I began to see the mistake. Did I believe in chance? Was I believing that God was not providing for me right then? Did I feel that I was only half a person, needing to find the other half to be made whole?

Nothing brought the whole experience home to me as clearly as the story in the Bible of the man at the pool of Bethesda (John 5:1-9, 14). As I read the passage—"And a certain man was there, which had an infirmity thirty and eight years,"—I thought, mine's only thirty-six years, but that's fairly close. This unfortunate man was sitting by a pool where the traditional belief was that the first sick person to enter the water after the angel came (the water was troubled) would be healed. Similarly to the frustration of the man who always had someone beat him into the water, I was feeling like whenever a nice guy came along, some other woman would always win his attention.

I was sitting by the pool, crippled in my thought, thinking that I needed the angel to move the waters—or God to bring Mr. Right to my attention and all would be perfect.

When Jesus sees the situation and realizes that the man "has been a long time now in that case," you would think he would show some pity. But instead he asks the man a question. "Wilt thou be made whole?"

I applied this to my situation. Was I ready to see myself as already whole, as being made whole by God, not needing another person?

Like the man, I tried to evade the question and provide a pitiful argument. I don't have anyone to help me. No one introduces me to new people. It was too much like the Biblical account. "Sir, I have no man, when the water is troubled, to put me into the pool: but while I am coming, another steppeth down before me."

Jesus did not reply, "that's too bad, maybe I can help you get into the pool." He knew the power of healing was not in there. It was as if he ignored the man's argument, and said instead, "Rise, take up thy bed and walk."

It was a gentle way of telling me to raise my thought. I didn't need to be frantic. I needed to realize that God did not make me as half his child, but as whole, complete. I realized that I had to walk forward with this new found identity and not feel as if there was anything lacking in my life.

I decided to do as the man did. "And immediately the man was made whole, and took up his bed, and walked." I stopped seeing every male I met as a potential husband and began enjoying the company of all my friends, male or female. This change in thought did make a difference in my experience. Life became more enjoyable, and less anxious.

The new approach became so natural that two years later when I was on a day-trip with two friends, my girlfriend said to our friend driving, "You should marry Kim." His reply was, "Okay, do you want to marry me, Kim?" My husband is that friend and we still laugh at his odd proposal that I accepted. We've been happily married for 16 years.

* *An earlier version of this story was published in the Christian Science Monitor*

Inner Trust & Faith

Dorie Hanson

"Do you know that you are the temple of God and that the Spirit of God dwells in you."
1 Cor 3:16

I don't know if you would call it faith or intuition but whatever it was, I needed it. Being the middle child of a large family, I had to be on the alert. I never knew when a big brother was about to play a prank on me, but with the help of that sixth sense, I'd move in the right direction at the right time. You'd saved yourself one more time . . . or was it someone or something else that saved me?

You've probably heard of the "still small voice" within. It seems almost mysterious, but, when it starts happening to you much of the time, that's when you say, "I'm the lucky one." What's really happening is that you are open to listening from within. You have discovered that is where the wisdom lies—and now you think you have a secret.

How does this help you as you grow up and enter the big world? First, you realize that you're not alone. When you have a problem, you take it within yourself to get your own answers—answers that work. Now, no one talks you out of the thing you really want. You know that you are connected to higher power and you feel special. No one can take that away.

You see around you, those who feel greater or lesser than you, and you set your goals to take the high road. You get the job—the one you really wanted and you can't stop smiling. You live in two worlds at once. There is the physical world outside of you, but the best world is the one that lives inside of you—where home and security is.

Then one day, an opportunity comes along that can change your life. It's all about giving up that lucrative job and trying out your wings. It's about the challenge of using your own resources to create a new way of living. Is it scary? Kinda. It's new, and when you check it out with your higher power within, you're covered with goose bumps. You've had that sign before, so you know you are on the right track. But now you have to rely on that inner trust and faith like you've never had to before and you realize that all those earlier experiences of following your inner guidance was to get you to where you are today. To get to that place of trust and believing in yourself and your ability to create your own destiny.

Feeling secure that I had guidance from within, for the next ten years I experienced what few jobs could ever have given me—a chance to see the world and move to a higher level of consciousness. I became sharp—to hear without ears, to see without eyes, to feel without touching. The world had become my playground and I would never go back to the old ways.

I had discovered this incredible power within me, which became my roadmap to a joyous and prosperous life. So call it faith, or intuition or God. No matter what you call it, when you hear that still small voice within, take heed. Trust it, and live the life you were meant to live.

Adventure out beyond your fears
through forests lush with trembling tears
go hand and hand with faith as guide
and Self's true friendship at your side.

from Sept. 2000

I'll See You Again

Angela Jenkins

"It is the Spirit who gives life." John 6:63

I am 46 years old now and still miss my mother terribly. My younger sister and brother and I grew up in a fairly nondescript old farmhouse in Prince Edward Island. My father was a Baptist by birth only, my mother an Anglican and a very quiet religious woman. Living in a rural area with one unreliable car meant we did not always get around.

I can remember the well-worn Bible my mother had as one of her most precious possessions. I would see her read it at times and when she would get cross at us, the word "Ye" would be one of the things we would hear: "Ye children get in here!" It was as if she was reading passages right out of her Bible as she scolded us.

As we three children grew up, we surpassed my mother in height. She was a petite thing—barely 5 feet tall with a tiny build. Still, when she held the Bible and talked to us, she was so full of confidence, we all felt she was seven feet tall.

A strong belief in God is what my mother instilled in me. We couldn't get to church often, but my mother made sure we said grace before mealtimes and that we said our prayers at night. We grew up in P.E.I. on meat and potatoes. I guess we were poor, but as children didn't really notice. Before eating a meal, our mother would always lead us with a short grace. She always closed her eyes, but I remember keeping mine open to peek at her. She looked very serene as she said, "Thank you Father for these blessings which we are about to receive and make us truly thankful." I was usually thankful if it wasn't fish we had to eat.

I also remember as a young child being taught the simple prayer at night of, "Now I lay me down to sleep, I pray the Lord my soul to keep and if I should die before I wake, I pray the Lord my soul to take." Our mother made sure we knew there was something up there that was larger than us and could take care of us in times of need. Lord our God. Lord our Father.

Our mother also made sure that we always had nice Easters, and Christmases and it wasn't just because of the Easter Bunny and Santa. It was because we were all together laughing, playing cards and having fun. The grace would always be longer at those times, and my mother would often talk about the true meaning behind these two religious holidays.

Our mother really personalized God in our lives. At times, she talked about Him as if He was an invisible member of our family—always present when we needed him.

On March 1, 1991, my father and brother were killed in a terrible water accident. My father was 53 and my brother only 21. The time after their deaths was very sad for us. My mother kept up a stoic face for my younger sister and me, but we could tell her heart was full of pain. In her grieving, she would visit their grave sites often, but she was never mad at God for the accident. She kept going to church as often as she could, but since her diagnosis a few years before of Multiple Sclerosis, her mobility was poor.

In late February 1993, almost two years to the day after the passing of my father and brother, my mother was diagnosed with terminal cancer. The doctor told her she had four to six months to live. Our mother was determined to take care of her financial matters as best she could before her passing, and told me that it wouldn't do to die in six months —that she had to live at least until January 1 of the next year to take care of matters the way she wished.

When I found out my mother had terminal cancer, I was 28 years old and living in Montreal with my husband and 9 month old baby. I recall going to my boss and telling him I had to go home to stay and be with my mother as I would not have the chance to do it next year. I packed a suitcase and took my daughter Sarah to Prince Edward Island. My mother was elated. Dying and elated—what a contradiction. She was so happy to have her first grandchild at her side.

As the months passed, my mother's health deteriorated. I remember days before her death when someone came to visit her at the house and had talked at length about a problem, my mother said to me (after they had left) "that is her cross to bear, not mine." My mother had to conserve the little energy she had left, as her time was coming to an end.

Although my mother was very weak, she insisted we still have Christmas and celebrate Christ's birth. Since she had taken care of all her financial matters, she no longer cared if she would make it to January 1. A couple of days before Christmas our mother went into the hospital for the last time. I remember the visits I made and always, when I left, I said, "I'll see you later Mom."

On Boxing Day, I was at the hospital and one of my aunt's had also come home to P.E.I. to be with my mother. As I left the hospital room that day, I turned to my mother and said, “Good-bye Mom.” Subconsciously, I knew, and within the hour after I left the room, my mother passed with her sister at her side. She was only 51.

My mother did not fear death. She knew without a doubt that she would be going to meet her Maker, and see those she loved that had died before. She was especially looking forward to seeing my father and brother again.

I believe my mother’s grace was simply an extension of the grace of Our Father—who art in Heaven. I do miss my mother and one day I shall see her again.

Meanwhile I can still hear her voice saying those well-known words:

“Our Father, who art in Heaven, hallowed be thy name, thy Kingdom come, thy will be done on earth as it is in Heaven. Forgive us our trespasses, as we forgive those who trespass against us. Lead us not into temptation, but deliver us from evil. For thine is the Kingdom, the Power and the Glory, for ever and ever. Amen.”

Tight between the mountains peeking
star of wonder points the spot
where the day's last dawn lies weeping
for our future — freed yet caught.

from Jan. 10, 1987

Gloria
In Gratitude
for Bringing us
all together
[illegible] 2010
Virginia LoneSky

The Power of Faith

Virginia LoneSky

"If you have faith as a grain of mustard seed . . . nothing shall be impossible to you."
Mt. 17:20

These inspiring words from Jesus, came into my life when I was ten years old. I didn't understand their full implication then, or how it would serve me fifty years later, but the way they came to me was in a prize. I won a shiny charm bracelet for memorizing twenty New Testament verses at Vacation Bible School. The passage was written in small print and encased in glass, which contained one tiny mustard seed. The chain has long been lost, but, for two reasons, the orb is still one of my most prized possessions.

First, because it is the only surviving treasure from my childhood. My parents separated when I was five, and I moved around from relative to relative until I was twelve. And second, this passage has given me hope and strength to never give up.

During any bleak situation, I found I could change circumstances by praying and believing things would change. Whenever I felt lonely or sad, I would look at that bracelet and say the passage. But as a child, I wondered, "Why a mustard seed, and how does it give you faith?"

It wasn't until I was in my teens that I realized it was an analogy of the unwavering faith a small mustard seed must have—trusting, and never doubting that it would grow and become a plant. I could only hope to find that kind of faith in this lifetime

Then, in my fifties, I did. A sudden series of life-changing events pushed my physical body into total immune system shut down and debilitating pain. Tests were inconclusive, and, with it acting like several different diseases, doctors couldn't pinpoint what it was. I could barely stand up or walk, let alone function in a working capacity. Nevertheless, since I was my only means of support, I had to go to work. Prayer and gratitude got me through each day. Although my body was weak, my faith kept my spirit strong. I made myself envision only a positive outcome, and spoke only positive words. This went on for nearly three years.

Ironically, I experienced many blessings in this state

of pain and suffering, not feeling like a victim, but knowing that, sometime we need to test ourselves. Not as a punishment, but to see if we believe in our own abilities to transcend realities as Jesus said we could.

I was also given insight that sometimes the experience isn't just for us to grow, but for others in our life to grow too. Nonetheless, the pain was exhausting, and I finally realized that the doctors I was seeing had done all they could. So after three years of no results, and with a good heart, I prayed the most powerful, connected prayer of my life—that the right doctors would come into my life . . . now!

Within 24 hours, I thought of three friends to call. I asked them for the names of Naturopathic doctors they knew, and chose one. While being treated, that doctor asked me what I was going to do about *that*, and pointed to my painful wrist.

I said, "Well give me the name of a doctor." He did, and to my surprise, it was a doctor in mainstream medicine, who would be using pharmaceuticals. I thought this would be a real test of facing my fears, but in prayer I heard, "This is drastic. You MUST get help immediately." I prayed again and heard, "You are beyond what Naturopathic medicine can do for you." A warning I took seriously.

At my first appointment, I found this new doctor very caring and comforting. After running tests, he had several answers, and I realized I didn't have to forfeit my beliefs. When he gave me a verbal diagnosis and the side affects of the recommended medicine, I never spoke it back, I never thought about it, I never owned it. I just listened to the protocol, prayed, and made my agreement with God. I decided to take the pharmaceutical for ninety days. My faith took over from here. With every daily dose, I prayed, putting intent into the medicine to only do good, and let all else fall away. I asked God to magnify the positive affects of the medicine, as I realized somewhere there was a scientist who had developed this to do good for people.

Within thirty days, I had let go of all my fears, and my inflammation levels went from 110 to 8. My doctor was amazed. I still had a long way to go, but my recovery was clearly ingrained in every prayer.

Having faith to direct the positive outcome, expecting miracles and Divine intervention each day, I stand today, fully functional, without any debilitating pain, and without any dependency on medication. I have come through the dark night of the soul, into my spiritual rebirth, one more time. I know that your faith can be tested but it is never a punishment. It is so you can see how much you can do when you really believe you can move mountains.

The reward this time, for having remembered scripture, was in receiving two of my most precious prizes. Not in the material realm, but in the birth of my grandchildren, Katherine Emma and Julianne Olivia—two new shiny and bright little stars, which I contain in my orb of love. As a grandmother, I can pass forward, to a new generation, all my life's lessons, and His legacy. "*If you have faith as a grain of mustard seed . . . nothing shall be impossible to you.*"

In this Now of never ending
as you tend your day's bright bloom
is this present we are sending
through your fragrant afternoon

from Conversion 1987

As love reclaims its purpose
hope redeems its place
within the heaven's vastness
upon your smiling face,

and in your never ending dream
of peace for all and each
we gather in your quaking
we touch within your reach.

from Singing Stars

Marion Mahoney

Albert's Angel

Marion Mahoney

"And the Angel of the Lord appeared to him."
Judg 6:12

I was close with my twin sister's husband, Albert, and before he died I had asked him to send me a sign so that I would know he was all right. Albert was buried on June 3, 2002. Three months later to the day, on Sept.3, 2002, I was sitting on my deck in the late afternoon talking to him and asking him if he was okay.

The day was beautiful and clear. Then I looked up and there in the sky, was a single cloud in the shape of an angel. I called for my daughter, Micki, who came running and then grabbed her camera. The cloud lasted only long enough for her to capture the picture. As the cloud disappeared, Micki and I felt a breeze blow past us. I believed it was the sign I had asked Albert to send me, so I knew he was okay.

I thank God for sending this sign. I reproduced the photo, which appears on the cover, to share with you in hope that it give you comfort, knowing that our loved ones are always close by watching over us.

Rest now in your struggle's clearing
a meadow's stop along your way
gather knowledge fast about you
pick life's flower from each day.

from Mystical Verses

Waking Up

Laura Masciangelo

"For whoever shall call on the name of the Lord shall be saved." Ro 10:13

Every one has a story to share and every story is unique, with their own inspiration or lesson. Knowledge is power and can help us get motivated to move in the right direction. With that in mind, I wish to share my story for everyone to learn what and how I felt in surviving an intense, life threatening ordeal.

All day, on Friday the 13, in June, 1984, I half expected something dreadful to happen. Nothing did. . . until the evening. Although, I believed in God, I was uncertain about my faith. I worked at home, as an accountant, and was busy working and setting up my business. That night, I was just finishing up some paper work. My only child—a boy 7 years of age—had long gone to bed. So at 1:30, I put the books away, and sleepily fell into bed. It couldn't have been more than five minutes later when my head turned into a hot burning fire of pain. It was so severe it felt as if someone had put an axe into the dead centre of my brain.

I must have made a noise, because my son rushed into the room crying, "Mom you're breathing terribly. Please get up. I'm scared."

I tried to get up, but could hardly move. I managed to stand for a moment, and remember yelling to my son to call 9ll, just before I felt my body drop to the floor.

Bless his heart, he did just that, and I was glad that I had taught him what to do if anything should happen to me.

The ambulance came for me and took my son next door to my friend's house. Upon arrival at the hospital they said I had the flu, and to make a long story short, they sent me home in a taxi . . . with me in bare feet, clad only in my nightdress.

The next day I went to my family doctor who sent me right back to the hospital with a phone call saying to check my brain. He suspected something was drastically wrong. He was right. There was something terribly wrong. A procedure, called a spinal tap, would find out if blood was leaking from the brain down to the spinal cord.

I remember praying to the Lord and asking for his help. Strangely enough, I somehow knew that this was meant to be. But my main concern was for my son, Jason. He had just became captain of his soccer team, and was so happy about that. Now I felt it wouldn't happen for him because of me. His father and I were divorced, and he lived far away with his new partner. As it happened, their baby was born while I was having a life saving procedure, so he wasn't any help in getting Jason to his games.

The doctors, on finding blood in my spine, which had come from my brain, concluded I was having a brain hemorrhage. The neurosurgeon said it was a weak blood vessel that had burst, calling it a brain aneurysm, and that I would need an emergency brain operation.

One of the doctors said, I hope all your papers are in order, because most probably you won't survive."

As they wheeled me into surgery, I said, " I can't die. I have to finish raising my son and I haven't started on my children's story." As doubt of my survival rushed in, and being very upset, I added, "I came here to relievc a headache, not to have brain surgery."

I was glad that I had told my sister, Maggie, that if anything should happen to me, to finish raising my son. Feeling so helpless, I continued to pray to God. In desperation, I made deals, pleading with Him to let me live as I wasn't finished with this world.

The Lord was calling to me, "Do you believe in Me, do you have faith?" I knew then He was my salvation. Whatever he could do for me, I just knew He'd do it. My faith and love for him was so strong now, that I knew I'd be all right.

When I was under the operation, one of the Lord's angels told me to "follow this white light and you'll be back on Earth." No matter how hard it was for me to get back on Earth—and it was hard—I knew the Lord stood beside me. What I didn't know, until later, was that I had a stroke in the middle of the twelve hour brain operation. After that I was in a coma, which lasted almost three months. Things looked pretty grim for me.

The doctors told my family that, although I survived the brain operation, I was still comatose. This is where prayer, faith, hope and love came to my family. They took turns from morning, all through the night to the next morning, never leaving my side. For three months, they took shifts, always by my side, keeping me stimulated, and praying for me to remain alive. This I believe is why I'm alive today and ready to produce a book that I hope will be an inspiration and a learning tool for others.

The Lord, and my family's prayers and strength kept me from dying. When I woke up, I was able to join in with my prayers and my gratefulness in surviving a thirty percent chance of living.

Would you believe that worst day of my life was the best day? For it was a new beginning. My prayers and the prayers of faith and hope of the many people who loved me, for which I so gratefully accepted, had become a reality. Thanks and praise to God that I was able to finish my son's upbringing and to write my children stories.

My son is now thirty-three years old and I'm blessed with two grandchildren. The children stories are here too, but I have many more outlined to write. Typing with my good hand and the use of one eye, I'm managing to write a book of someone surviving brain surgery and living to write about it. And the best part of all is that I have a wonderful partner in my life, enjoying with me the goodness of God's precious love.

Praise be to the Lord.

Within this moment's longing
as minds-in-motion dance
the stars begin their singing
beneath the full moons glance.

And in the candles lighted glow
the vapors of your voice
ascend, converge, convene unseen
above your joyful noise.

from Singing Stars

Trust in the Lord

Susan Muldoon

"Trust in the Lord with all your heart,
and do not lean on your own understanding.
In all your ways acknowledge Him,
and He will make your paths straight."
Prov 3: 5-6

My husband and I were unable to have children of our own and after seven years of marriage we adopted a nine year old girl. At the time of the adoption we were told that our daughter had a full blood sibling, a sister, five years younger, who was still living with their birth family and therefore was not available for adoption. We advised the social workers that we would be willing to adopt the younger sister also, should she ever need to be adopted.

The following three years were, not surprisingly, very

difficult as we adjusted to being parents and our daughter adjusted not only to losing her birth family, but also to her new adoptive family. She had suffered greatly, and her pain resulted in very challenging behaviours which drained us, stressing us to our limits. I often struggled to understand why we had to endure such hardship.

Then, one Sunday, I found the above scripture verses on a magnet at church. I brought it home and stuck it on the fridge door. It became my mantra. I read it every morning at the start of my day and at those times when I was feeling particularly tired or low. It never failed to uplift me, to remind me to trust and not be afraid. This helped me greatly to parent my daughter, to see beyond her behaviour and to envision her as a strong and beautiful woman in the years to come.

Over those years, our daughter never stopped missing or worrying about her younger sister. In spite of our efforts, and the efforts of our social worker, we could not obtain any information on the younger sibling and her welfare.

Four years passed and my husband and I decided that we would like to adopt again, but given that our daughter had a little sister out there somewhere we felt that we should adopt a boy. Our social worker assisted us in completing the second adoption application and, in due course, we were advised about a number of young boys who needed a forever family.

There was one boy in particular that we felt we would be able to accept, but before we could pursue our interest, I became ill. I lost a lot of weight, became very weak, very tired and depressed, and I needed a number of weeks of bed rest to regain my strength. I remember one day lying in bed feeling particularly low, when a good friend, who is also my prayer sister, came to visit. She told me that there was a reason for my illness and that God had something great planned for me. I remember responding, quite indignantly, "Then it better be good!" I simply could not understand why I had become so ill at such a critical time in the adoption process.

With the love and support of family and friends, and my family doctor, I slowly regained my health and strength and my mood gradually improved. I had feared that due to my illness, the boy that we felt able to accept, would by now have been adopted. However, that was not the case. He was still available. We met with his social worker who felt that we would be a good match for his needs and we began to plan a first meeting with him in his foster home. His social worker had decided not to say anything to him about us until we confirmed the date that we would visit.

We arranged to speak with his social worker on a Monday morning. However, the Friday before, we had received an unusual message from a social worker who worked at the same agency from where we had adopted our daughter. We decided to call her first and when we did, we got a huge surprise. Our daughter's little sister had been in a foster home for fourteen months and would likely become a crown ward, needing an adoptive family. The social worker wondered if we would be interested in adopting her. In shock, I laughed and my husband cried.

"Of course, of course," we kept repeating, but "of course." After a lengthy conversation, we agreed to meet, and I put the phone down. A minute later the phone rang and it was the social worker for the boy. Still in shock, we shared our incredible news with her. She was so understanding and reminded us that she had not told the boy anything about us so that no harm had been done.

Within a few weeks, as anticipated, the younger sister did become a crown ward and needed to be placed for adoption, and we agreed wholeheartedly to accept her. As soon as it was possible, the sisters were reunited after not having seen each other for almost four and a half years. What a joyous miracle. I could barely breath as we drove to the foster home for the reunion.

A month later, the younger sister was placed with us and since then the sisters have been slowly adjusting and reattaching to each other and we are adjusting to having two daughters.

My prayer sister was right. God had indeed something great planned, not only for me, but for my husband and, most importantly, for these beautiful sisters. I am so glad now that I got so sick and was unable to adopt earlier in the year. I did not understand then that our second daughter was waiting, and I had to be kept out of commission until the time was right.

I now have no need to keep those scripture verses on my fridge as they are—and will be—forever firmly stuck to my heart.

Your million mirrored smiles are spreading
flowing forth to finally claim
our reflection — your true image
seen at last to be the same

from Conversion 1987

To calm the quaking core of knowing
as you face your greatest fears
we will catch— in every rain drop
all our trembling truth-full tears.

from Aug. 16, 2004

A Mother's Cry

Brenda Murray

"Lo, I am with you always." Matt. 28:20

As a young married woman with six children under ten years of age, including a set of twins, I periodically experienced depression and exhaustion. My husband worked all day at the office, plus, at night and on weekends, farmed our land. I did my best to care for everyone and enjoy motherhood. I was proud of the role.

Sometimes, however, circumstances got out of control. I was feeling depressed, I needed sleep, I cried over the smallest occurrence and found that coping was next to impossible. With my energy so low, my ability to function was severely compromised. Even the simplest duties were overwhelming and my family was feeling the brunt of it. It was a challenge for me to prepare meals, do laundry and household chores. I was also unable to meet my family's emotional needs, and found it difficult to give my children the care and loving support they needed for their growth and development.

On one particular day, it came to a crisis. I asked my husband for relief. Would he care for the children for a few hours while I rested? They were acting out and squabbling among themselves, further adding to the stress. I took this as an example to mean that I wasn't handling the dynamics of the household very well. Unfortunately, instead of agreeing to support me, he became angry. Raising his voice, he listed off the many chores that he intended to accomplish that day and that it was most definitely not possible for him to do as I had asked. I would have to come up with another plan.

It was the last straw. I felt isolated, helpless and desperate. My thinking wasn't clear—I only knew that I could not go on living this way. My thoughts spiraled down, down, down. I had to escape. I had to get away. Even suicide crossed my muddled brain.

I ran from the house and into a field near the barn, where I knelt down in the long grass and, in my misery, called out for help—for strength to carry on. Had I left it too long? Should I have been asking for strength all along? I wept, as I shared my life and my concerns with God. I opened myself completely, exposing all that I held inside.

Gradually, a peace fell over me, and as I sat quietly

afterwards, my thoughts became clearer and my emotions steady. After that day, I found that I was better able to refocus my energy on my goals of homemaker and mother and thus put to use my talents of nurturing my family. My tired feet were refreshed.

The work of raising my children was important to me, plus it was work for God, by creating healthy, happy, loving people who would give back to the world as a reflection of the care that they had received.

". . . He inclined to me and heard my cry. He drew me up from the desolate pit, out of the miry bog, and set my feet upon a rock, making my steps secure."

Ps. 40:1-2

Accept the terms of living's grace
that ticks and talks beyond your trace
its magic is your heritage -
delight to cross illusion's bridge.

from The Unison of Circles

Just Believe
Allison Nolan

God, Grant Me the Serenity

Allison Lynn Nolan

"Be of good courage,
and He shall strengthen your heart."
Ps 31:24

For over a year, I had been on an emotional roller coaster that drained me in many ways. I not only battled with the break up of my marriage of 17 years, but also battled alcohol.

The split with my husband was not the result of my drinking, nor was it the cause. As I looked back over the past years, I realized I'd had a problem with drinking for a lot longer than I thought. I had been trying to find happiness in myself for some time, and I wanted to be honest with my husband. When I told him that I no longer felt the same way about him as I once did, this started a long and bumpy ride. It was a ride I did not enjoy.

A friend took me to my first meeting of Alcoholics Anonymous where I heard the Serenity Prayer. "God, grant me the serenity to accept the things I cannot change, the courage to change the things I can, and the wisdom to know the difference."

I had read that prayer before, but never realized how important it would be to me and how it would help me in my struggle. It took eight months for me to admit that I had a problem with alcohol. Once I did, however, I got myself on the right path, even though over the months I slipped and fell.

When I got weak and fell off track, I would pray for the strength to get up and try again. At first I thought I could only ask for help so many times, but each time I asked, I felt a peace come over me and I knew I was granted serenity. It took many questions and many more prayers to realize the things I could change and those I could not.

My husband blamed himself for our marriage ending and I tried to help him realize that it was not his fault. I was not happy and didn't want to live a life with regrets and resentment. I finally accepted that I couldn't change his thoughts nor could I change him. The only thing I could change was me. With that intention, I started anew. All I needed now was courage.

One day when I was walking my dog on the trail near our house, I was feeling very sad and down. I remember asking God for courage—the courage to fight the demons that were taking over my thoughts and my emotions. That is when the second line of the prayer made more sense than it ever did before . . . but I needed the courage to change those things that I could change. Something within me told me that I had the power to change my addiction but I needed help more than I had ever imagined. I was afraid of failing again. Every time I thought I was on my way—the right way—something would happen that would send me spiraling downward.

At one of the meetings, someone said, "Where there is fear, there is no faith." It made so much sense to me. How could I be afraid when I have asked God for help? Did I not have the faith to know all I had to do was ask? This is where the wisdom came in. I now needed to learn what I had control over and what I did not. There was a difference, and I was starting to see it. Every step was laid out for me. Each time I learned one step, I was handed another, until it all fell into place, right where it was supposed to.

I still struggle with my addiction and things are not settled with my husband, but I am able to deal with things a little easier and I have learned a lot about myself in so many ways. I know there is a plan for me. I know that prayer is powerful. I pray and give thanks everyday for what I have learned. I needed to trust in God and now I have faith that he will open pathways for me to follow. It is much easier to handle the stresses in my life as I know my prayers are heard and they are answered when the time is right. I do not question when or how the pieces will fit. I have learned to Let Go and Let God.

I needed, I asked and I was given. God granted me the serenity, the courage and the wisdom, and for that I am grateful.

We would wrap our gifts in pleasure
Tie your hopes in ribboned blows
fill your life with wisdom's treasure
proofs your self so surely knows

from Sept. 1987

We Are One

Alberta Nye

"For He Himself has said, 'I will never leave you nor forsake you.'" Heb 13:5

The setting sun cast pink and orange streaks across the Hawaiian sky and I was embraced by the warm emerald waters as I floated on the undulating waves. Breakers foamed onto the beach about a hundred yards away from me. My skin registered a gentle breeze.

It is rare to experience a moment that is so perfect. I looked up into the sky and felt at one with All That Is, the God of my Being. Indeed, I felt so connected and loved, that I said aloud, "I feel so peaceful right here and now that I could swim with a shark and know that I was safe because we are all One."

Not two minutes later a man came running down the

beach yelling. I saw his outstretched arms and just caught the end of what he was saying — "a big fish swimming your way."

A friend, swimming with me, streaked by on the way toward the shore yelling, "Swim! Swim!"

I noticed that there were others heading for shore as well but, in my state of calm, I felt no urgency.

I looked off to my left and saw the mottled grey fin of a Tiger shark sticking straight up out of the water . . . and heading in my direction. Part of my mind registered that it was a shark while another part laughed and said, "Oh look, God has sent me a shark to swim with." I felt not one iota of fear.

As I watched, the fin disappeared under the water. I hung straight down in the water in my black bathing suit. Hadn't I heard somewhere that sharks mistook black suited swimmers for seals? There was a part of my physical self that was trying to make me panic—to go into fear mode—but deep within myself I knew there was no need. Somehow I knew that I was safe and that this shark was sent to show me that I could trust my connection with God.

I turned around and saw the fin behind me, pointing in my direction. By now it was about eight feet from me so a quick calculation told me that the nose was maybe four or five feet from my body. Yet, I still felt no fear. I could feel love pouring out of me toward the shark and I felt it being returned. We weren't afraid of one another, just interested.

Meanwhile, people on the beach kept yelling at me to swim in. They didn't know that I was not in danger. After an eternity of one or two minutes of facing the shark, I turned to make my way to the shore. Just as I did that, a surge came and gently pushed me forward. Having turned my back on the shark, my physical self realized that as I stretched out to swim, my feet would be inches from the shark's nose. But again, that other part of me knew that I was safe.

I arrived on the shore to the relief of the frightened group of people waiting, and as I walked out of the surf, I turned back to the ocean. The fin was still there, pointed toward the shore as if seeing me safely in. As I looked out and sent another message of love and thanks, the shark did a U turn and disappeared below the surface.

It didn't reappear. I smiled inwardly and thanked God for the reassurance that, "I am always with thee. I will never leave thee nor forsake thee."

To this day, I carry that experience with me, knowing that I am never alone.

In fair exchange we come invited
summoned at your own command
so herald the joy in right redemption
through your power to understand.

from Aug. 16, 2004

Filled With Light

Gloria Nye

" To give light to them that sit in darkness . . ."
Lu 1:79

I was devastated when my father died, at the age of 84, after caring for him in my home for six weeks. Many times in his life, he had told my sisters and me that he would live forever, so when he died, I was battling, not only abject grief, but anger at him for lying.

Three weeks after his passing, I experienced an incredible happening, which changed my life forever. One Saturday morning, around 10:00 o'clock, the whole house was strangely quiet. I lived in the third floor flat with my 6 year old daughter. On that particular morning, she had gone to a friend's house to play, and the two rambunctious dogs and their owners, who lived downstairs, had gone to the market. The radio played quietly, and with the lack of usual Saturday morning hub bub, I became even more acutely aware of my misery. My whole body ached with pain until I thought I could bear it no longer. I lost it, and crumpled to the floor, sobbing. Then from somewhere deep inside me, I cried out, "God, help me."

After a few moments, I pulled myself together and went to the bathroom to wash my face. I still felt hopeless and helpless, and as I looked into the mirror, I wondered why I had called for God's help, since I was an atheist. I used to call myself a Happy Atheist, and at University I would hotly debate with the theology professor about the existence of God, challenging him to prove it, which, to my smug victory, he could not—at least not to my satisfaction. I dried my face, and since I was feeling so miserable anyway, I decided to vacuum— a task I didn't enjoy. I barely got started when suddenly the vacuum turned off. I sensed someone standing behind me and I thought my daughter had come home and had playfully turned it off. I swung around, but no one was there. I checked if the plug was in, which it was, but the switch was off.

As I stood there, wondering how it got turned off, I became aware of the presence in the room growing bigger and stronger. I felt apprehensive because I couldn't see anyone, but I knew, without any doubt that someone—or something—was in the room. Then, I heard the music coming from the radio. It was a flute solo that my father used to play. Astounded, I lowered myself slowly into the big overstuffed chair in the corner. (It was the corner where my father's hospital bed had been set up.)

With my father's familiar flute music filling the room, I sat, stunned, as this incredible and luminous—beyond white—light appeared in the opposite corner. It grew to a large egg shape that shimmered and glowed. I kept blinking my eyes to see better; it was as if I had other eyes that were seeing it. Then I saw—or sensed—an incredible being standing in that brilliant light, and my father beside it. Immense, total, unconditional and indescribable love filled and then emanated from the whole corner of the room.

I rose in awe, with my mouth open. The knowledge that a higher being really did exist flooded over and through me. Then, a liquid stream of the white glowing light poured out of that radiant corner, across the room and into my open mouth. I felt the light coming in, flowing down my body, filling every inch, every cell, each tiny part of me and spilling out through my toes and finger tips. Then it filled my head and overflowed in a fountain of light. It was the most incredible experience of my whole life. As I stood there, in this exalted state, I somehow knew the answers to everything, and it was all so simple. I turned and looked to my left and then my right, and although I sensed only a straight line, I knew I was part of an infinite circle. Of course, I thought. We *do* live forever. All time is now, without end. It was all so clear and obvious.

I don't know how long I stood there. I wasn't aware when the flute solo ended, or when I sat down. I wasn't even aware when or how the power and the glory in the corner of the room dissipated.

Gradually, however, the room returned to normal, but when I looked around everything had changed. I lifted my arm and touched it lightly with my finger tips, marveling at the incredible beauty . . . the wisdom . . . and amazing intricacy of my body. I went to the window and looked out, marvelling at once ordinary things. Everything looked different. The trees sparkled with life, even the sidewalks seemed alive—everything was imbued with an inner invisible light.

A few minutes later, my daughter came bubbling home, followed by the downstairs couple and their barking, leaping dogs. I gave them all a hug—even the dogs. They all looked so precious and wonderful. It was as if I was seeing them, and the world, for the first time. I felt like a newborn baby with adult faculties.

In the weeks that followed, I must have seemed like a crazy person. I had to contain myself, because I wanted to shout from a mountaintop that God was alive and that those Sunday School stories, the Bible, and other sacred writings were true. I went to church, and smiled, seeing the light around many of the people. They knew. They knew.

It has been forty years since that experience, but the memory never fades. The light lives on within me and when I leave this physical form I will see it and be with it again. When my father died, I was angry that he had lied to me. But after that Saturday morning, I knew what he meant. He had indeed spoken the truth. We do live forever.

There is no message gone unheard
unspoken — broken from your word
for from your promise we have come
to light time's smile within Earth's sun

from The Present or Running Away

Through the sunlight's crystal prism
drawn beyond the earth's green reach
entwined in every human calling
what we once ourselves beseeched.

from Jan. 11, 1987

A Second Chance

Cindy Otter

"The Lord is close to the brokenhearted and saves those who are crushed in spirit." Ps 34:18

My name is Cindy. I am 45 years old, and have been with my husband for 13 years—married for 10. Our relationship started rocky. At the time I met my husband, he had three children and was not yet divorced. He did, however, manage to get his divorce within the first year of our dating. His children were still very young, so gradually I was able to grow a strong relationship with them, regardless of the negativity we received from his ex-wife. These wonderful children are now part of my life and are very much my children as well.

At the beginning of our relationship we had a lot of problems. We drank a lot on weekends which led to fighting and arguing. Regardless of these problems, however, two years after we met, we were married and managed to have a somewhat stable life—or so we thought.

But then the day came when there was nowhere to go but down. We tried counseling and talking but after years of trying to fill our lives with material things, I couldn't do it anymore. I left my husband and, after ten years of marriage, we separated.

Before I left, I talked to my friends and family about my situation. My sister had been going to church for about four years and in one of my really down times, I phoned her. She came and picked me up and we went to the park to talk. That day she prayed for me and I gave myself to Christ. Since then I have attended church every Sunday.

I hadn't been on my own for over twenty years and even though it was scary I was excited to start a new journey. I knew I would never go back to my husband, and I looked forward to a new life ahead of me.

The first couple of months were wonderful. I enjoyed my new found freedom—coming and going whenever I wanted—but it was short lived. I started to feel empty and lonely. Even though I had been going to church for about four months before I left my husband, it didn't seem to be enough. Then my sister told me about an Alpha course—a world wide program—that was offered through the church. In two weeks, when the course became available, I joined. Through this course, and through the grace of God, I found direction, peace and fulfillment in my life. I began to change my way of thinking, acting and living to a more positive, productive way. I also made many friends that are now my Christian family. These are people whom I can count on for support if I ever need anything, or just need to talk.

Everyone around me noticed the difference in me and the new positive way I now looked at life. My husband and I kept in contact and things were changing between us. He also noticed a big change in me, and by my changing, he was also changing for the better. We were now really communicating for the first time in years, and I was falling in love with him all over again.

Within eight months my husband and I got back together. One Easter weekend, he decided to come to church with me on a special Good Friday service. At the end of the service, the Pastor asked if anyone wanted to give themselves to God. To my amazement, my husband went up to the front. What a delightful surprise! Right there and then, he declared his faith and gave his life to Christ. I was so overwhelmed with joy, I couldn’t stop crying. Now my husband has also joined the Alpha course, which I have volunteered as a helper, and he regularly goes to church with me on Sundays.

I'm not saying that we never argue anymore or that we don't fight with our own personal demons sometimes, but I do know this—we would not be back together, seeing a future for the two of us if it was not through the grace of God blessing us with a second chance. We know that there are going to be ups and downs, and that's okay, because now we know, as long as we put God in the middle of our relationship and our lives, we will be able to conquer anything that life throws at us.

It's one thing to know of God but it is life changing to have a relationship with our Father. There is nothing on earth that can't be done through God.

Praise God and bless you all!

Within our whisper, roar and rhyme
minds explode and stars align
new worlds rejoice— and time begins
again to beat like angels' wings

from The Present or Running Away

God's Grace

Kathy Roberts

"I can do all things through Christ who gives me strength."
Phil 4:13

At the age of thirty-five I felt blessed to marry a man whom I thought had a connection to God that was similar to mine, and I looked forward to our companionship in Christ.

For the first few months things went well but then my dreams began to shatter. My husband became verbally abusive and started using drugs. Things continued to deteriorate and finally ended in him agreeing to go into rehab. As much as I struggled financially and emotionally while he was there, I was pleased that he was getting the help he so badly needed.

During my husband's absence I prayed for wisdom and guidance, knowing that I couldn't handle it alone. That was when the miracle happened.

Although I was faithful with tithing to my church, finances were so tight that, on one particularly bad week, I considered not tithing. I struggled with this as my need for groceries fought with my devotion to God. After much prayer and spending time in His wonderful presence, I decided to tithe, as I knew that God would look after me in my time of great need and according to his will.

I felt calm and assured as I headed to church, my envelope in hand. I deposited my envelope and while there met a woman in the foyer whom I had met a couple of times before. I didn't know her well and was surprised when she handed me an envelope. Upon opening it, I found a Thanksgiving card along with a gift certificate of $100 for our local supermarket. Praise the Lord! The woman explained that as she was praying that morning, God had told her that I needed help. I would never doubt again. God is with me and will never forsake me, just as He has said.

I continued with my prayers as my life was still in turmoil and I was having difficulty focusing on what needed to be done. God spoke to me time and time again in the middle of the night, prompting me to read scripture. It was always the very thing that I needed to hear or read during my struggles. Just as I was feeling almost overwhelmed, God prompted me to read Psalms 46:10 “Be still and know that I am God.”

In the following week, I saw that verse in five different places so I know that my Heavenly Father was trying to tell me something. At that point, I surrendered everything to Him and left all the issues that I was facing at the foot of the cross.

After six months in rehab, my husband returned, and stayed with a couple from the church until I was ready to accept him back into my life. He did move back in, but soon started the verbal abuse again. Within two months, I knew he wasn’t going to change and that I had to end my marriage. I had lost my job due to the recession, and finances continued to plague me but my prayers to my Heavenly Father also continued and I knew that God would provide. I had some lady friends pray with me that my husband would find a place quickly because I could not think about spending another day with the abuse. We also asked that He would send someone my way to help with my apartment and to share the expenses. Again, He delivered very quickly.

The following morning, my husband came home after a night shift and told me that he had found a place and that he would be moving out. That very same day, my pastor’s wife called me and told me that there was a lady from the church who was looking for a place to rent. I got in touch with her and she was very interested in sharing my apartment and is now my roommate. To add on to that, God has filled my life with amazing friends that pray, encourage and love me.

I have this indescribable peace within and know that He is my source. I have become actively involved in my church and am helping out with the Alpha ministry. I am happy to share my story with others and see people grow and be richly blessed just as I have been throughout the past two years.

Looking back, I realize how much He delivered peace, joy and love—opening doors where they needed to be open and shutting doors where they needed to be closed. Had I not remembered to praise God through the storm, I have no idea where I would be today but I don't think I would have had the same outcome. Praise be to God.

Takeoff in Newfoundland

Wally Rooke

"In God I have put my trust, I will not fear."
Ps 56:4

During the 1960s I was an engineering-journalist for a Maclean-Hunter weekly trade magazine, *Heavy Construction News.* My principal duty was to travel to each province at least once a year, seeking out and reporting on new and different construction techniques on projects across the country.

An episode during my first visit to Newfoundland was one of my more memorable moments in all my travels. I had just completed a road tour of the western part of the island where they were pushing through the Trans Canada Highway to replace the legendary Newfie Bullet railway across the province. I was flying down from Deer Lake to Stephenville to check out a project.

The regional airline in those days was Eastern Provincial Airlines, which used a fleet of Dart Herald aircraft. Their propeller-driven planes had wings above the fuselage—not blocking the view—and great for flying over interesting terrain.

An important detail to note is that there were thirty-six available seats on the plane and a netted cargo hold near the only entry door at the rear. Because the wing was overhead, passengers just had to step up two or three steps from the tarmac to enter the plane. The stewardess stood outside, next to the door and viewed our boarding passes as we got on.

I was assigned the seat in the second last row, in front of the rear exit where we had just climbed aboard. With the last passenger seated, some of us near the rear door could hear a conversation between the stewardess and the pilot who had returned from the snack bar of the small Deer Lake terminal.

This was in the days before computers and apparently the check-in desk had issued a total of thirty-six boarding passes to passengers, all of whom were already buckled into their seats.

The stewardess then alerted the captain, "This aircraft is licensed by Transport Canada to carry only thirty-five people. How do we decide who has to get off?"

The captain's response was to double check the netted cargo area nearby for any especially heavy luggage or tools, etc. He must have decided that the extra passenger would not be a weight problem because he told the stewardess to come aboard and close the door.

Both of them then made their way up the aisle to the cockpit, disappearing through the door in the bulkhead, which separates the passenger compartment from the flight deck.

As we began our taxi out to the end of the runway, the fellow in the seat behind me—a dishevelled unshaven Newfoundland miner on his way back to the Labrador mines with a little too much to drink—unbuckled his seat belt and swayed his way to the front.

Standing with his back to the bulkhead, he raised his arms, as if in prayer, and announces in a loud but somewhat slurred voice, "Ladies and Gentleman. This plane is overloaded. But trust in the Lord. We'll get off the ground!"

Then, like a choir master, and all the while the plane was taking off, he led us in a rousing rendition of *Onward Christian Soldiers.* Once the aircraft was aloft, he stumbled back to his seat and, for the remainder of the flight, proceeded to drone Irish laments.

The stewardess and crew—out of earshot behind the bulkhead—had no idea of the divine intervention so heartily invoked during that momentous lift off.

You who hear that different drummer
march united bound for peace
'cross the heart's most sovereign landscape
down its alleys — up its streets

Thronging through its verdant valleys
ringing out across its plains
we have heard your call for learning
coursing homeward through your veins.

from Peace Makers 1986

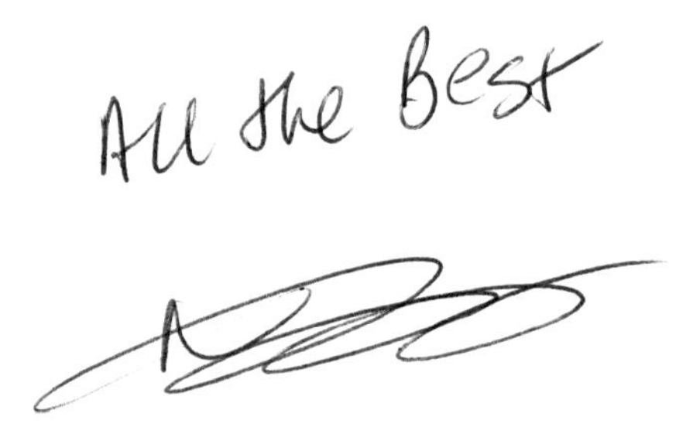

Heavenly Encounters

Nancy Rorke

"For he will command his angels concerning you to guard you in all your ways."
Ps. 91:11

When I was four years of age, I met Jesus. Before that, I never even knew his name as my parents were agnostic.

One July morning, my older sister Diane and I ran down the hall of our apartment, excited to be allowed to play outside. We started to take the exterior stairs from the third floor to the ground.

"The first one at the bottom will be crowned the winner," Diane yelled. She assured me, that with her being the oldest and the smartest, she'd be first.

"But I want to win," I said.

"If you climb down the balcony, you'll beat me."

I hesitated for only a moment. *My sister wouldn't lie to me, would she?* I climbed onto the top railing and stretched my arms out around the concrete pillars. Two moves down, I sensed danger. There was no place for my feet on the pillars. Energy rushed through me, my heart pumped, and my body trembled. With a sense of dread, I yelled to Diane, "PLEASE HELP ME!"

My sister froze, and time stopped as I fell backwards, arms stretched wide like Superman. Everything went black before my tiny body collided with the ground.

When I opened my eyes, my neck was arched upwards towards the sky with my right arm crunched beneath my back. Pain seared through every part of my broken body. I fainted.

It felt like hours later when I opened my eyes but it was probably only minutes. I squinted at the hot sun. To the right, a woman hovered above the ground. Her bare feet glowed. I looked up past her silver dress, sparkling in the sunlight. She spread her silver-tinged wings for me. "Don't worry, Nancy." A smile touched her serene face. "You're going to be all right. I promise you."

I fainted from the pain again, but this time I visited Jesus in heaven. We were in this beautiful garden and I sat on His lap and watched the other children playing. When I awoke, the angel was still there and comforted me, but she disappeared when adults arrived to transport me to St. Joseph's Hospital. I fainted for the third time.

When I awoke the next time, I saw a woman dressed in black and white and I felt scared. I'd never seen a nun before. She explained that she needed to take x-rays to see my injuries.

The hospital wasn't like heaven. I knew it couldn't be a good place, with its shiny bed and horrible x-ray machine. Where was Jesus and the other children? I remembered the pure love and light that emanated from him to all the children and I couldn't understand why I wasn't allowed to stay with him. The joy of being with Jesus was better than anything . . . even chocolate ice cream.

After this encounter, I loved Jesus with all my heart and I began to pray to God. However, as a result of my childhood fall, I was plagued with intense migraines, making my life miserable.

Fifteen years later, on a sunny cold icy day in February, I met another angel. Across the street, Barbara, my ride, waited for me. I slid down my icy driveway onto the road right in front of a fast moving station wagon, wide-eyed in anticipation of the inevitable impact. Silently, I spoke to God. "I'll see you in heaven today."

But that was not to be. I felt strong invisible arms pick me up and gently place me on the neighbour's lawn. The driver of the station wagon insisted that he take me to the hospital since he was sure he'd hit me. I assured him that he hadn't.

He shook his head. "That's impossible."

Overwhelming joy flooded my heart and soul.

Barbara said, "Why are you so happy? You could have been killed."

"God loves me. It's a miracle."

Another miracle occurred on a warm October morning in my twenty-seventh year. I was walking down the stairs with my baby in my arms when I lost my footing and began to fall.

"O my Lord," I cried silently. "Please help me. Take my life but spare my baby. Let me fall without harm to her."

Instantly, I was placed upright against the wall. Momentarily stunned, I thought I must have imagined falling. I grabbed the railing and continued walking carefully down the stairs.

My husband stared at me, his mouth open. "What just happened? One minute you were falling and the next minute you were vertical."

When I explained, he smiled. My faith in a God who answered prayers became as strong as steel.

In my middle years, the Lord brought me to heaven again. I'd developed severe abdominal pain and on February 23, 1996, while sitting in church, the pain became so excruciating I thought I would die.

My husband told me that I stood up, screamed, and fainted. A member of the church, a paramedic, wanted to call for an ambulance but my sister-in-law, a nurse, intervened and took responsibility for my health.

I found myself outside of a library in heaven. Seeing angels dressed in brown monks' robes, I thought I was dreaming. They shook their heads and spoke telepathically. "You cannot enter heaven; you haven't finished your mission. You have to go back. We will heal you, but you must promise to complete your task on earth."

Twenty minutes later, I awoke in church healed of the abdominal pain that I later believed was appendicitis. On reflection, I've never understood why the angels didn't also heal my chronic migraine pain that had persisted since my fall of so many years ago.

Although I still had migraines, this encounter infused me with a zest for life, and I practised daily meditation along with prayer. Feeling more and more inspired, my lifelong dream of becoming a writer became my priority and my life was filled with joy and contentment.

Five years after my last encounter, another one of God's earth angels, my friend Gloria, e-mailed me a link to a website that she thought might help. I checked it out and it turned out to be a life saver. After forty-seven years of enduring excruciating pain from weekly migraines, I had finally found relief and it would be amiss of me if I didn't share the source. Perhaps someone reading this, can also be helped at www.watercure2.org.

I feel so privileged to have experienced these heavenly encounters from an early age. These encounters with God's angels have transformed my life, and I know, without any doubt, that God will command his angels to safeguard us always.

Magic spark of cell-bright splendor
will and wonder coalesced
you are truth's eternal tender
of the living flame of peace

from Peace Maker 1986

Genessa Tonin

Forgiving Friends

Genessa Tonin

"Behold, children are a heritage from the Lord."
Ps 127:3

My name is Genessa, and I'm 9 years old. When I was 8, me and my friend, Maya had a fight. She said that I was being mean but I thought that she was. I was really upset and talked to my mom about it.

The next day I said a prayer (our Father). After that, I admitted to Maya that sometimes I was mean. She forgave me and I forgave her, and we were friends again.

We go to the same school, St. John in Guelph, Ontario, Canada. This year we are both in Grade 4 and in the same classroom. We are still friends and like to go swimming together.

I got an award for Humility because my teacher picked me out of my class.

My school motto is on the wall in the main hallway just outside my classroom door. It is:

C	Christian & Friendly
H	Humility
R	Respect
I	Integrity
S	Service
T	Team Work

Hold fast to the silver thread
spun by your becoming

from Broken Bits of Grace

Loving Hands

Trina Virgin

"For the Lord will be your everlasting light,
and the days of your mourning shall be ended."
Is 60:20

The unexpected happened to our family several years ago. An anguish no parent should have to go through. I lost my faith that day and was angry at God.

It was very early Sunday morning on September 9, 2001, when a policeman told us that Matthew, our 19 year old son, had been rushed to emergency. We raced to the hospital, calling family on the way. We had no idea what to expect when we arrived. The news was bleak. He had been hit by car after leaving a party and had suffered serious brain trauma.

As I sat in a small room surrounded by family, listening to the doctor, I felt I was in a nightmare and wanted desperately to wake up. I could not believe what I was hearing and slipped into a state of shock. Something inside me took over and I went on auto pilot to function.

Matthew was unconscious and on life support. The doctor suggested surgery. We agreed, hoping for a miracle. That night we left the hospital to collect personal items from home so that we could stay by our son for as long as possible. The doctor cautioned us that if Matthew did regain consciousness, he would probably never live a normal life again. At the time, I thought the worst. I just couldn't comprehend my son living in a vegetative state, needing total care for the rest of his life. I prayed that night that somehow the doctor's prediction would be wrong.

The next morning, sitting alone by my son's bed, the nurse came in and told me the doctor would be in to talk to me soon. A sense of dread enveloped me. Something had changed from the day before. It was a subtle difference—a combination of things—the odour in the air or that the very energy around me had shifted somehow.

When I held my son's limp hand, his presence was not as strong as it had been. It was difficult to pinpoint exactly what it was, I just had an inner knowing, an overwhelming gut feeling and I told the nurse I already knew what the doctor would say—that we had to let him go. She had tears in hers eyes as she squeezed my arm, and left without saying a word.

Our son had had a stroke during the night and it was time to say our goodbyes to him. On September 10, 2001, our dear son, Matthew, passed away from this earth.

I was not the only one who grieved so terribly. My husband, our oldest son, grandparents, our siblings, our friends, my son's friends—each carried a sadness that was hard to express. The pain was almost unbearable at times. We each had to find a way of dealing with our loss. It was evident, by how many people attended his funeral, that Matthew had touched many lives.

For a long time after that, I was angry with God. Those following months were filled with difficult dark days and I fell into a deep black hole. I had asked for help and it did not come—at least not in the way I expected. I did not see at first that I was being offered help, because it did not come in the way I wanted. What gave me the determination and faith to carry on, was the love and support of people around me, even strangers, who also loved our son and missed him. I truly felt I had many loving hands supporting me.

Slowly I knew I had to climb out of the darkness towards the light and it was an effort. I asked for help and guidance, but I also had to learn to listen for it and to pay attention for when it came. I believe that God sent me who and what I needed to get through this awful period. I do believe we are given a choice how to respond to things that happen to us and I chose to move forward instead of staying in that wounded place. I forgave all who were involved in my son's accident—but most importantly, I forgave God and myself for doubting Him.

Now in the most unexpected circumstance I meet people who tell me their stories of grief and somehow I am able to comfort them by offering a loving hand of support. The Lord has ways of changing our plans and the miracle I asked for was not the one I got. The miracle to me, was the outpouring of unconditional love given by so many people. I have grown so much since and I am grateful and blessed to help others as I once was.

Your answer is this moment's bliss
beyond what words can ever say
accept your view and joy in this
that outshines sun's forgotten day

from The Present or Running Away

Authors' Biographies

Valerie Bannert, author of *A Promise Kept,* was born in 1928 to a loving family of 3 brothers and 2 sisters. That love was stretched somewhat when she joined the Roman Catholic Church and stretched somewhat greater when she entered the convent. After 25 years in a Religious Congregation, a different path called to her. "The path was deep and dark and difficult on one side, yet deep and bright and meaningful on the other." After spending many years in an ecumenical community, in 1981 Valerie joined with others members to establish Eramosa Eden—an ecumenical retreat centre. How she found the right location is the subject of her story

Diane Bator, author of *Gifts from God*, was transplanted from Alberta to Orangeville in 2004. The married mom of three boys, she chose to bloom where she's been planted and has rekindled her passion for writing, photography, and painting. She joined the Headwaters group in April 2007 and appears on their website www.owg.netfirms.com. She also writes song lyrics for her father Joe Rondeau, a musician in Alberta and struggles to keep up with the laundry.

George Brooks, author of *My Mother's Angel,* is a retired school teacher and has published children's stories and educational material. He recently won first prize at the *Writing Out Loud* contest sponsored by the Muskoka Arts Council (Ontario). Check out a news- paper article at www.almaguinnews.com and search "George Brooks brings Tusker to Life."

Lisa Browning, author of *Ask, Believe, Receive,* received a Bachelor of Arts in English from Toronto's York University in 1988, and subsequently worked as an editor for over fifteen years. Having recently rediscovered her passion for writing, she has had essays and articles published in a variety of online and print magazines. With experience in both the public and private sector, with small companies, nonprofit organizations, and major corporations, Lisa currently manages a freelance writing and editing business, with a goal to inspire others to create and maintain peaceful and well-balanced lives. She can be reached at lbrowning@rogers.com

Michael Butler, author of *Someone Was Watching Over Me,* is a retired broadcaster who worked in radio and television for over 40 years as an announcer, reporter, producer and editor. He was born in Birmingham England 64 years ago and lives in Guelph Ontario with Beverley McAleese, his partner of 27 years. They share the house with Maggie (his dog), Rooster (her parrot), and Shamus and Paddy (their cats). Michael has two beautiful grandchildren

Elizabeth Paddon Copeland, author of *Just Ask,* is a performing artist / educator who has worked within a variety of different spiritual communities over the last 20 years—Christian (United, Catholic, New Thought) Buddhist and Pagan—working to strengthen faith connections using song, poetry and drama. She also facilitates Lay Reader's workshops—supporting congregants to share their faith through scripture. She believes strongly in what Matthew Fox talks about— that all spiritual traditions are wells drawing from the same river. She lives happily in Bark's Falls, writing stories and songs with her husband and two cats.

Ruth Cunningham, author of all the poems, is a seeker, a listener, and a visionary. She was born in Kelowna, B.C., and has worked and lived in B.C., Alberta, Sask, Ontario, and Washington State. She now resides in the Ontario countryside between Cambridge and Guelph, with her husband George, and until recently their 21 year old cat, Min, who is now frolicking on the other side. Her personal life story is bound by her work with the Speaker Material and its Self-self life study. As a line from one of her poems goes: " . . . I cannot tell where I end and you begin . . ." Ruth's poems were taken from her book *Mystical Verses*. To order this, and to read more of her wonderful poetry, go to her website at www.self-to-self.com or email her at spinfo@golden.net.

Lynn Emerson-Walsh, author of *The Triumph of the Human Spirit,* lives in Anacortes, Washington with her husband and ninety-five year old mother. Lynn has published several articles including: *The Beginning of a New World Paradigm, A Search For Deeper Meaning at Christmas, The History and Spirit of Crone,* and is in the process of writing a book called, *Treat the Cause, Not the Symptoms.* The focus of this work is to explore the root causes of physical, emotional, psycho social, mental, spiritual and electromagnetic imbalances and time-tested natural remedies. This book is the culmination of several decades of study and investigation, personal life experience, and the latest research.

Helga Farrant, author of *A Nest of Cardinals*, is a lover of God and His inspiring creation. She recently moved from Milton, ON to Calgary, AB and enjoys responding to the call of the majestic Rockies and hiking along the rivers. She has been involved in Christian work, both in a full-time and volunteer capacity, for many years and has a special interest in seeing the nation of Rwanda recover. She has a Master of Theological Studies, and life's circumstances have also taught her about the great depths of the Father's love and nurture. She is the proud mother of two, and has two beloved little granddaughters.

Kathy Grandia, author of *Little Boy Pebble,* came to Canada in 1974, is "mostly a mother," and is married to Ken who is a big help, especially with her computer. Her parents have just celebrated their seventieth wedding anniversary and blessings abound in her life, starting with healthy children, the most wonderful of grandkids, good health, eyes to see, ears to hear and a mind to use with caution and continue to develop toward wonder. Her husband says, she can often be found, "cutting a perfectly good big piece of fabric into smaller pieces and then sewing them back together." "An activity which makes little sense to him," Kathy notes, "but he is the first one to settle many evenings under his quilt with a good book. Good friends make life sweet, and laughter is a most welcome companion. To God be the glory!"

Kim Sherman Grove, author of *Searching for Mr. Right,* is a freelance writer who likes to share thoughts with others. She has been published in *The Toronto Star, Watershed Magazine* and *The Christian Science Monitor.* She believes in the power of prayer in all aspects of life.

Dorie M. Hanson, RNCP, CNP, author of *Inner Trust and Faith,* for 20 years has traveled throughout North America, and to Great Britain, Ireland, Scotland, Australia, New Zealand and the Caribbean, lecturing and consulting on peoples' well being. Dorie has spoken at School Boards, Day Care Centres, Community Centres, Chiropractors, and at Wellness Weekends. She owns her own business, carrying a line of natural health products, and safe home and personal care products. "I am passionate about empowering others to take charge of their life and their health."

Angela Jenkins, author of *I'll See You Again,* was raised in a small rural community in Prince Edward Island, the oldest of 3 children. A true Maritimer at heart—no matter where she is—her Newfoundland mother and P.E.I. father (with salt water in his veins) brought her and her siblings up to live by the Ten Commandments and the Golden Rule. "One thing I believe strongly, is that the faith we have in God, Lord, Allah, The One will sustain us during times of loss and heartache."

Virginia LoneSky,ThD, author of *The Power of Faith,* is an Ordained Minister, Shamanic Ceremonialist, Healing Practitioner, Labyrinth Facilitator, Lecturer, Writer, and Founder of Peaceful Endeavours Labyrinth Ministry. She lives in Southeastern Michigan. Visit her at www.peacefulendeavours.com

Marion Mahoney, author of *Albert's Angel,* is a twin, one of ten children, and married Mike Mahoney, a professional hockey player, who has passed away. They have 4 children and 8 grandchildren, whom she spends much time with, singing, dancing and doing shows. Marion hosts students from all over the world who remain life long friends, and her house is usually full of people with celebrations of fun for any occasion. She is a member of Knox Church, and the Guelph Chapter of IODE. Loving angels so much, she was not surprised when one appeared in a cloud to her. Marion also enjoys traveling, meeting new people, reading, gardening and music.

Laura Masciangelo, author of *Waking Up*, was born in Sudbury, Ontario, May 6, 1953, to Italian parents, raised in Toronto, and received her accounting certificate at Humber College. With 8 siblings, a mother, and a father in and out of hospital, Laura learned about sharing. Separated and with a young son, after brain surgery, she had to learn how to read and write all over again, and began writing children's books. After raising her son, she traveled to Australia to learn illustrating, and met her life partner. However, after eight years, and wanting to be closer to her son and his family, they moved to Acton, Ontario where they now live with the 3 animals they brought back with them. The 2 tabby cats, mother and son, (Marbles and Oscar) hate the snow, and the miniature fox terrier, Sara, thinks she's a human being. Laura would welcome any editing or publishing help in bringing her story of her brain recovery into book form. (519) 853-1270 or laura.masciangelo@gmail.com

Susan Muldoon, author of *Trust in the Lord*, is the youngest of eleven children, and was born and raised in the town of Drogheda in the Republic of Ireland. She emigrated to Canada in 1987 and has lived in central British Columbia, Nunavut (then the Northwest Terrorities), and now Ontario. Susan believes in the transformative power of sharing our spiritual experiences and is delighted to have a personal story of the strengthening of her faith included in this collection.

Brenda Murray, author of *A Mother's Cry,* is a retired nurse with specialty in occupational health nursing. She divorced in 1991, and her six children, now young adults (3 married), are all successfully contributing to society. Brenda has four grandchildren, and lives in Port Stanley, Ontario.

Allison Nolan, author of *God, Grant Me the Serenity***,** is 44 years old and own a dog grooming business that she runs from her home near Mount Forest, Ontario. Recently separated, she still has her dog, Max. Writing and journaling helps her release emotions and thoughts. "I now write daily whether it is a poem, a story or just a few thoughts jotted down. I love being outside, especially in the woods—a wonderful place to go for inspiration or just a little peace."

Alberta Nye, author of *We Are One*, has been on a spiritual path since she was 22 years old when she had a life-changing, near-death experience. Mother of three, grandmother of two, Alberta lived in Hawaii for seven years where she co-produced a documentary, *One God, Many*

Faces. She nursed her ex-husband for six weeks, before his death, and this, coupled with her close personal connection to All That Is/God, has led her to writing, filming and producing her own documentary— *Smiling at Deat*h - A new look at death and dying.

Gloria Nye, author of *Filled With Light*, and editor of this book, is a mother of one daughter and grandmother of three. She lives at the Eramosa Eden Retreat Centre, with her sister, Alberta. Gloria co-authored The *DreamQuest Dictionary* and the *DreamQuest Cards* (www.dreamquestworld.com). Two of her short stories respectively received honourable mention and third prize at The Eden Mills Writers' Festival, and Words Alive Literary Festival. Watch for the release of her novel, *Dragonfly*—a story of two women, living in different worlds and times, linked by an ancient dragonfly brooch.

Cindy Otter, author of *A Second Chance,* was born and raised in Guelph, Ontario, with three older sisters. Their parents were very loving and raised all four children with proper morals and values. Their father passed in 2001, and their mother continues to stay strong in supporting them in mind and spirit. When Cindy is not working, she loves swimming, going to the beach and camping with the family. Now that her own kids are older, she and her husband enjoy getting away by themselves—even if it's just to quietly watch a sunrise, a sunset or a gentle rain.

Kathy Roberts, author of *God's Grace*, was born and raised in a little outport town in Newfoundland, and after 30 years, moved to Ontario for employment. She loves life, enjoying nature, camping, walking, cross country skiing, and the simple things, and tends to spend as much time as possible with family and friends. "I think they are the most important part of living, besides having a relationship with our Heavenly Father of course."

Wally Rooke, P.Eng., author of *Takeoff in Newfoundland,* is a Winnipeg consulting engineer specializing is concrete technology. Since his travels in Newfoundland, he's worked on civil engineering projects from Kuwait to Cairo, Rio to Puebla and Trinity Bay to Tsawwassen. He's recently taken on the happy role of grandpa.

Nancy Rorke, author of *Heavenly Encounters,* has been published in *The Globe and Mail*, *Sideroads of Dufferin County*, *The Top Ten Joy Journal* and *Charting a Course for JOYful Living*. Nancy is a member of the Headwaters Writer's Guild in Orangeville, and writes for their blog. http://headwaterswritersguild.blogspot.com She lives with her husband of forty years, her daughter, granddaughter, three rescued homeless cats, two dogs (one saved from a pound) and a rabbit. One of the cats was black, and since black cats were rarely adopted, Nancy said to her husband, "I believe they find us. It's part of God's plan and we're meant to keep him." They call him Parker as in Peter Parker, aka Spiderman, because one night he got out and they couldn't find him, until they heard a plaintiff meow at their bedroom window. Parker had scaled the brick wall all the way to the second floor. Nancy can be reached at njd411@yahoo.com

Genessa Tonin, author of *Forgiving Friends*, is nine years old and lives in Guelph, Ontario. She loves her ballet and hip hop lessons, and swimming with her grandmother, Gloria Nye. She has two big brothers, two cats (Leo and Sparkle) and two loving parents. She wants to be an actress when she grows up.

Trina Virgin, author of *Loving Hands,* lives in a small rural community with her husband, two old cats and a feisty little dog. She enjoys her work with developmentally challenged adults, and to relax, she loves love to read, write and garden. "That's me in a nutshell."

NOW the day of excavation
this the task of every soul
to discover its creation
this the truth you each extol
from Conversion 1987

Notes

Notes

Notes

Made in the USA
Charleston, SC
06 March 2010